Introversion & Leadership is aimed at leaders wh[o have a] preference for introversion (whether identified [through a] system such as Myers Briggs or just from their o[wn self-knowledge]), and who may feel that introversion is a disadvantage with the expectations that often accompany a leadership role. The book would also be of interest to those who coach, manage or support introverted leaders.

What are the big questions answered?
What is introversion anyway?
Can I still be a highly effective, impactful leader without pretending to be more extroverted than I really feel?
What strengths can I leverage as an introverted leader?
How can I feel comfortable and confident with my natural leadership style?
What strategies can I use to overcome the challenges I face in the workplace as an introvert?

Rachel Anderson began her career as a forester, managing trees and woods, but realised over the years that her real fascination and talent was in helping people to grow, rather than trees. Rachel established her coaching and consultancy practice Tea & Empathy Ltd in 2008, and since then has coached over 1000 executives on a one to one basis, and countless more through workshops and group coaching. Practical, pragmatic and empathetic, Rachel helps people to accept and appreciate the person they really are, and in doing so opens the door to them realising their full potential. She describes herself as a 'social introvert living an integrated life', combining running a successful business with raising a thriving family.

Rachel writes about change, personal and professional development, and coaching in her blog at www.teaandempathy.com.

She still like trees.

Introversion & Leadership

Practical Strategies for Being at your Best

Rachel Anderson

a TEA & EMPATHY book

Copyright © 2020 Rachel Anderson

All rights reserved.

ISBN-13: 9798657187366

CONTENTS

1 Preface 1
2 What is Introversion? 2
    2.1 What do introverted leaders look like? 2
    2.2 Introversion and extroversion: why should we care? 2
    2.3 Where it started: personality types 3
    2.4 The Myers-Briggs Type Indicator (MBTI) 4
    2.5 Differences in the brain 4
    2.6 Are you an introverted leader? 5
3 Myths and Stereotypes 8
    3.1 What makes an ideal leader? 8
    3.2 The extrovert ideal 9
    3.3 The problem with the ideal 9
    3.4 Busting the myths 10
4 Uniquely You 14
    4.1 Your introverted preference 14
    4.2 What does an introvert look like? 14
    4.3 There is more to personality than introversion 15
    4.4 Leveraging strengths for leadership 16
    4.5 Strengthening yourself 20
    4.6 Helping others 20
5 Day to Day Strategies 23
    5.1 Managing energy 23
    5.2 Leading others 26
    5.3 Meetings 28
    5.4 Presentations and public speaking 30
    5.5 Networking and socialising 31
    5.6 Office environment 32
6 Working with Extroverts 35
    6.1 A word of warning 35
    6.2 The value of extroverts 35
    6.3 Diversity as a winning formula 36
    6.4 Nurture who you have 36

	6.5	Communicate your own needs	38
7	Pitfalls and Watchouts		41
	7.1	Overplaying your strengths	41
	7.2	Don't box yourself in	44
8	Conclusion		46
Acknowledgements			47
Where next…?			48

1 Preface

Somewhere between a third and one half of people can be described as introverts, but in business and particularly in leadership roles it can often feel that the more extroverted traits are to be desired, developed and rewarded. Even office design seems to support and encourage extroversion but makes the introverts among us less comfortable and have to work harder to stay at their best. The result? Often a gradual undermining in confidence and almost a sense of shame in not being a natural outgoing, gregarious or a 'larger than life' leader. Some leaders become closet introverts, covering their natural self with a public leadership persona more in line with expectations, but maintained at huge energetic cost and often stress. Others find it hard to accept their introversion as they believe some of the myths and misconceptions - "I often enjoy being sociable, and like people - therefore I can't be an introvert", but then struggle to understand how to maintain their energy levels and effectiveness over the long term. This book aims to explain exactly what introversion is and is not; to help introverted leaders understand how to leverage their strengths and become the very best version of themselves.

2 What is Introversion?

2.1   What do introverted leaders look like?

Claire is a Head of PR. She shares an office with two other people. She regularly chairs meetings and addresses conferences. Her days are stacked with appointments and regular interruptions from her team. Every day when she gets home, she's grateful to pour herself a glass of wine, put on some music or pick up a book, and unwind.

Peter is the MD of a global coaching business. He manages a large team and a number of corporate client accounts. He has a desk in the studio, but often works from home, where he gets his best work done.

Lori is a photographer and runs her own business. She spends her days and evenings with clients in busy spaces: outdoors, at festivals or at music gigs, liaising with them about what they want and making it happen. She makes sure she schedules in a couple of days per week to get her paperwork sorted and re-charge.

All of these people are introverted leaders. Others include Barack Obama and JK Rowling. There is no single template for an effective introverted leader, or any restrictions to what they accomplish.

What they have in common is a preference for introversion: they feel more at home with their inner selves than the external world. They boost their energy by having quiet time. As Lori puts it:

"I would describe introversion as being more insular – I value time alone and like to consider things carefully."

2.2   Introversion and extroversion: why should we care?

The rise of personality profiling, self-help and popular psychology has brought the terms introversion and extroversion into common language. But what do people think about them?

Oxforddictionaries.com – top of the google rankings for online dictionaries - defines an introvert as 'a shy, reticent person', while an extrovert is 'an outgoing, socially confident person.' Popular definitions like these maintain a culture that finds extroversion desirable, and introversion somewhat lacking. Certainly, in leadership roles, whether in business, public office, or the local community, you would expect to see a confident person over a shy one.

Yet these definitions are inaccurate and unhelpful. Confidence is not related to introversion. In reality, the quiet, thoughtful power that introverts bring to their work is highly valuable; arguably even more so in a Western culture that is set up in favour of extroverted ways of working and thinking.

There is no reason why people more inclined to introversion can't be great leaders, but they may well be overlooked. Susan Cain argues in her book 'Quiet, The Power of Introverts in a World That Can't Stop Talking' that Western culture is set up for extroverts: success is associated with fast-talking, highly charismatic, sociable leaders who dominate meetings, act quickly and have a ready answer for everything.

Schools are set up to encourage active participation within a larger group, whether that's speaking up in class, activities at breaktimes, or extra-curricular clubs. It is this type of group-based, busy cultural infrastructure that plays into extroverts' hands – introverts succeed in spite of this set up rather than because of it, often by putting on an extroverted persona. It doesn't have to be that way.

2.3 Where it started: personality types

Introversion and extroversion were first coined as personality traits in 1921, by Carl Jung. Following on from the work of two other eminent psychiatrists, Freud and Adler, he held that introversion and extroversion are characteristics that shape a personality, and that we are born with them. Introversion is a preference to turn inwards – to naturally be more comfortable with your own inner world, and extroversion a preference to turn outwards – to feel more at home in the sensory outer world. There are three crucial points about Jung's analysis:

Firstly, he held that while we are born with preferences, we are adaptable. We may have a preference for one-to-one conversation over large networking events, or vice-versa, but it doesn't mean we can't cope with or enjoy both.

Secondly, he saw introversion and extroversion as a continuum, rather than a black and white difference. Extroverts and introverts are not necessarily poles apart.

And thirdly, he believed that one preference was no better than another – indeed, that a healthy society or workplace needs both, and that to be healthy individuals, we need to embrace both sides, while being comfortable with our natural energy 'home'.

2.4 The Myers-Briggs Type Indicator (MBTI)

In the Second World War mother-daughter team Katharine Cook Briggs and Isabel Myers developed personality indicators based on Jung's theories, wanting to put them to practical use. Their handbook was intended to help the new female wartime workers identify jobs that would most suit them. Over the following decades, their work on the MBTI gained the support of many universities and the revised manual is still in use today, with workplaces and careers centres using the tool to help people understand their personal preferences better.

2.5 Differences in the brain

In the 1970s Hans Eysenck, a psychologist specialising in personality, proposed that introverts have more activity in the frontal cortex of the brain, and this explained why they preferred less stimulating environments. Scientific research over the past 15 years has given credibility to this assertion, by highlighting physiological differences between the brains of people who define as introverts and those defining as extroverts.

In her book 'The Introvert Advantage', Marti Laney describes the different pathways blood takes in the brains of introverts and extroverts. Participants in a laboratory experiment were injected with low levels of radioactive material so their neurological pathways could be monitored. Researchers found three important differences between the responses of introvert and extrovert brains:

1. More blood flowed to the introverts' brains. More blood in an area indicates more stimulation — scientists believe this shows introverts need less external stimulus than extroverts as they have more internal stimulation naturally. The right amount of busyness and noise for an extrovert easily becomes too much for an introvert, who already has a lot going on inside.

2. The blood of extroverts and introverts followed different pathways in the brain. The introverts' pathway was longer, taking in the frontal areas of the brain associated with problem solving and planning: introverts were focused on their internal worlds. By contrast, the extroverts' pathway was much shorter and flowed to the sensory parts of the brain: the extroverts were focused on the world around them.

3. The different pathways followed were linked to different neurotransmitters. The shorter, 'extrovert' pathway was the one used by dopamine, a neurotransmitter associated with movement and learning. Dopamine serves as a reward for new experiences. Introverts need less of this than extroverts: too much and they are over-stimulated. By contrast, the longer 'introvert' pathway is the one used by acetylcholine, a neurotransmitter associated with calm and memory.

These findings tell us that introverts are not simply 'quiet, retiring types' – they are people whose brains have a lot going on, all the time. The different ways introvert and extrovert brains work lend themselves to particular strengths. Introverted leaders can harness these strengths to become more effective in their work, rather than compete with themselves by trying to fit into an extroverted way of doing things.

2.6 Are you an introverted leader?

You may have a sense of your preference already. Remember that being an introvert does not necessarily mean you are shy or lacking in confidence - we will come to more of these myths later. There are a number of online quizzes that can help you understand your personality traits better (for example you can try the quiz at https://www.16personalities.com), but if you're short on time, there is one question above all that will give you insight into your natural 'home'…

"How do you like to re-charge your energy?"

If you had a free day to spend exactly as you wished after a busy week, and wanted to feel refreshed at the end of it, would you prefer to fill it with lots of social engagements and being out and about, or are you more likely to take a long walk, catch up with a close friend or curl up on the sofa with a book?

Of course, the answer will depend on your mood and circumstances, but *in general*, are you the sort of person that feels hyped up after a party or social gathering, ready for the next one, or do you feel in need of a rest?

Introverts will favour quiet situations and time to process, as their brains are wired that way. They tend to think deeply, focus, take time to consider things before speaking up, and prefer smaller, quieter groups. Too much noise or external stimulation is tiring.

What is Introversion?

Extroverts, on the other hand, prefer the outer world, their neural pathways reward stimulation. They get a buzz from talking to lots of other people; they are 'high energy' when out and about. Being alone or quiet too much is draining and frustrating for them.

The Myers-Briggs Foundation provides a comprehensive summary of introversion and extroversion http://www.myersbriggs.org/my-mbti-personality-type/mbti-basics/extraversion-or-introversion.htm.

If you identify as an introvert, and hold a leadership position, this book will help you make the most of the strengths your preference brings, and negotiate situations that are likely to be challenging. If you are an extrovert, this book will give you insight into your introverted colleagues, friends, and family, and help you work together better.

As we have briefly described, there are many popular stereotypes about what introverts are, and their suitability for leadership. We will examine these next.

Key Points

- Introverts recharge their energy from within, often preferring quiet spaces, while extroverts recharge through the external world.
- Western culture tends to empower extroverts, both through (inaccurate) popular definitions, such as 'confident' vs 'shy' and the set-up of many workplaces and schools.
- Jung was the first person to use the terms in psychology and believed both preferences were equal in value.
- Introvert and extrovert brains work differently, meaning they have different needs and strengths.
- Thinking about how you best replenish your energy will help you determine your own preference.

3 Myths and Stereotypes

3.1 What makes an ideal leader?

What words do you associate with leadership? What sort of person do you picture? Chances are you will conjure up someone charismatic, quick-witted and bold. Someone who's not afraid to speak and step-up, someone with ready answers, someone with a large circle of contacts and influence. Someone, who at first sight, falls squarely into the 'extrovert' camp. I'm guessing you're less likely to conjure up an image of a softly spoken, focussed, quiet type.

But what does make a great leader? It's a subject of great debate – with no definitive answers. Yet, some characteristics crop up again and again.

A survey of 195 leaders across 15 countries conducted in 2016 found that there were five behavioural themes that stood out. According to the research, strong leaders:

- Demonstrate strong ethics: they develop a safe and trusting work environment.
- Empower others to self-organise: they set clear goals but allow people to manage their time and working style themselves.
- Foster a sense of connection and belonging: they communicate openly and establish shared goals.
- Are open to learning: they set a work culture where people are encouraged to try new business approaches, and as leaders they are not afraid to admit mistakes.
- Nurture growth: they support people to develop.

The critical point about these qualities is that they are neither natural 'extrovert' or 'introvert' characteristics. Being the sort of leader who loves being where the action is does not mean you are more likely to excel at these behaviours. Neither is a quiet, more facilitative person. Both introverts and extroverts can be effective, transformative leaders. What's important is having the self-awareness and confidence to play to your strengths and understand your weaknesses.

3.2 The extrovert ideal

Susan Cain discusses how the western world has been dominated by an extrovert ideal over the twentieth century, particularly in business and public arenas. A culture of personality developed in which being likeable and able to conduct yourself with charisma were essential ingredients in getting ahead. This seems intuitive in the noisy, fast-paced U.S.A, but is also true of the UK, despite stereotypes of British fondness for queuing and being endlessly polite.

In the 1990s the Myers-Briggs MBTI assessment tool, used widely in universities and among employers, went through an updating and validation process in the UK and Europe. As part of the process participants were asked to share their type and their thoughts on ideal characteristics. 92% of people said it was 'better' to be an extrovert, despite only half of the population reporting an extrovert preference. Even among introverts, there is an assumption that it is better to be 'sociable', 'confident' and 'outgoing' – traits commonly associated with extroverts.

Introverts receive what Laurie Helgoe calls 'alienating feedback' all the time from society. These are messages we get, directly or indirectly, that the most successful way to behave is in the extrovert mode. We receive this feedback in phrases like 'the more the merrier', in looks of pity or surprise when we admit to wanting to stay in on a Friday night, and in work cultures that prioritise after-work drinks and networking as ways of getting ahead.

The danger with these messages is that we internalise them. We end up believing that the correct, successful way to be is to be one of the crowd, to prove your worth through partying, to work a room accruing contacts and success. And it is one way to be successful. But it is not the only way.

3.3 The problem with the ideal

Let's be clear from the outset that extroverts don't have the monopoly on being friendly, sociable or confident. Associating these positive character traits solely with extroverts does a disservice to all the sociable, friendly, confident introverts out there who also happen to have a consistent need for quiet, reflective time.

That point aside, the cultural preference for sociability, teams, and action assumes the opposite traits: contemplation, solitary working, and caution, are therefore less desirable. This assumption isn't just an opportunity missed; it can be dangerous. As Susan Cain puts it:

"Extroverts are much more likely to get really excited by the possibility of a reward, but because of that, they won't always pay attention to warning signals."

Ignoring these warning signals and not taking the time to reflect, can lead to major mistakes. Yet our education and work institutions reinforce the extroverted ways of doing things, with a focus on group or team working and brownie points for continuous active participation, regardless of the value of what is being contributed. Children are chastised for being shy or quiet, and schools offer little opportunity for happy alone time – the person in the school library or quietly at the edge of the playground is assumed to be a loner, worthy of pity.

What do we lose when society positions extroverts as the ideal leaders? We lose the strengths that introverts would bring to their leadership. Research by the University of Notre Dame found that extroversion was the primary predictor of whether someone would hold a leadership position. What it also found was extroversion wasn't an indicator that the leader would be *effective*.

So, while there is evidence to suggest extroverts are more likely to make it into higher paid, more powerful positions, this does not mean they are more suited to leadership than their introverted counterparts. The opposite may well be true: in a society that often overlooks quiet qualities, introverted leaders have the opportunity to make an important and unusual impact.

3.4   Busting the myths

There are a number of caricatures associated with both introverts and extroverts: introverts as pale, silent, bookish or geeky types, extroverts as brash, showy self-promoters. In reality, of course, we are all different - while some people might exhibit some of those characteristics, we've all got our own quirks, strengths and weaknesses. But the word association that goes with introversion is now long-held and damaging – especially when it comes to leadership. And words are powerful, the story we tell ourselves and others can create our reality. So, it's worth spending some time examining commonly held assumptions about introverts and checking how solid they are.

Introverts Are Shy
Google 'introvert definition' and see what comes up. Hopefully you'll find some psychological definitions, reminding us that introversion is a preference for turning inward mentally. But I bet the top popular definitions and synonyms include the word 'shy'. This is perhaps the biggest myth about introverts. Yes, introverts may

be shy. Just as redheaded people may be left-handed. But they are not associated traits.

In fact, some psychologists correlate shyness more strongly with extroversion than introversion. This is because shyness is a social anxiety – it is about wanting to connect but feeling worried or panicked about social contact. Introverts, with their preference for turning inwards, tend to be less anxious about social contact than extroverts, it's not as important to them. So, they may be quiet, they may be on the fringes of the room rather than at the heart of the party or conference, but they are happy there.

Introverts Are Anti-Social

It's easy to assume that because introverts recharge by having quiet time, they don't like people, or gatherings of people. While that may be true for some introverts, it is not the case for everyone. Many introverts enjoy parties, work events, conversation, and discussion. Many more introverts relish the opportunity to catch up with a trusted friend, or have a robust discussion about a work or political issue knowing they can focus deeply on issues that matter to them with people that matter to them.

But there are a couple of differences in the ways that introverts are social beings compared to extroverts:

Firstly, it's likely that introverts will need some quiet time to replenish their energy after sociable occasions. They are less likely to be heading to the after-party than their extroverted counterparts.

Secondly, because they are occupied with their internal worlds, it's more difficult to tell what's going on with introverts: at gatherings they are less likely to be wildly gesticulating and laughing their heads off. They may be talking quietly in a corner, having a great time but looking like they can't wait to get home.

Gill, an assistant director in university administration, tells of an introvert who felt very aware of how he came across:

> "He described how carpets are woven so there are rich colours and intricate patterns on the front. Yet the back looks plain and empty. And this conference delegate said that's what it feels like for him, as an introvert. All that colour and abundance happening in his head, but what most people see, at first glance, is the back of the carpet."

Introverts Lack Confidence

Similarly to shyness, lack of confidence and introversion are often associated in popular understanding. But this isn't necessarily the case. Introverts tend to think things through before they speak. And they tend not to speak unless it's important.

So, at meetings they can be quieter. But this doesn't relate to a lack of confidence, it's about a difference in processing information.

Introverts can often hold great confidence in what they think and say: they have invested time evaluating their ideas and share what they feel to be of value, rather than speak simply for the sake of it. This focus on ideas and principles rather than what everyone else is doing can create an independence of thought and quiet confidence that may elude the extroverts who are more attentive to what's going on in the room and keen to be in the crowd. Confidence doesn't have to be loud or showy.

Introverts Can Be Cured
We can all learn to modify our behaviour. Developments in neuroscience also suggest we can even re-wire our brains, by paying attention to different stimuli and responding differently. So, it is certainly possible to act more extroverted, to learn techniques to come across as more gregarious or lively than you really feel. Some of these are covered in later chapters. But that is not the point of this book.

Introverts do not need to change who they are to be effective leaders. To be at their best introverts need to embrace their preferences and their strengths. While holding a leadership role may mean introverts sometimes find themselves in situations they find uncomfortable, the same is also true for extroverts: where it might be the networking dinner at the end of a busy day that drains the introvert, it's more likely to be sitting at a desk to write the three year strategy that drains the extrovert.

There is nothing about your introversion that needs to be cured in order for you to become, and remain, an inspiring leader. But you do need to tune into what you are good at, and where you are weaker, so you know how to build an effective team and manage situations you find more challenging. This ability to understand yourself is where we turn next.

Key points

- The qualities of effective leadership do not belong to either introverts or extroverts, they are to do with having integrity, being authentic, and adopting an open mindset.
- In many western cultures introverts are bombarded with subconscious messages that they are unsuccessful or not doing things right.
- Over-emphasis on the extroverted approach can lead to harmful risk-taking and result in lost opportunities for talented introverts to take leadership roles.
- Introverts are not necessarily shy, anti-social, or lacking in confidence.
- While anyone can learn new skills, thought processes or behaviours, introverts do not need to be 'cured' to be good leaders.

4 Uniquely You

4.1 Your introverted preference

Introversion is a *preference*, not a fixed capability.

> **EXERCISE**
>
> Cross your arms in front of you.
>
> Now do it the other way.
>
> As you see, it's possible to do it both times, it just doesn't come as naturally the second time. That's how it is with preferences. You are absolutely capable of doing things differently if the situation calls for it.

So, for example, if you're required to attend a big networking event rather than meet someone over a coffee, you can. Or if you know your message is going to be better received in person or by phone, you'll show up, even if you usually prefer to communicate by email. We adjust our behaviours and approaches all the time, depending on our mood, our audience and what will help us achieve our objectives. Understanding which we prefer, and why, helps us prepare for situations we find more challenging, and play to our strengths when we can.

4.2 What does an introvert look like?

Figures from the MBTI test distributors suggest that the Western population is pretty evenly split between those with an introverted and extroverted preference. But the world doesn't divide neatly into two types of people: it's not always obvious whether your friends and colleagues belong to the introverted or extroverted camp. And even if it is, your introverted friends don't have the exact same personality as you. In short, there is no blueprint for being either an introvert or an extrovert.

The introversion/extroversion spectrum is broad – with people who are deeply and solely focused on their inner world at all times pegged at one extreme, and people who are constantly focused on the external environment pegged at the other.

Most people are somewhere in the middle – usually feeling more 'at home' with either the inner or the external world, but with interest and capability in the other side to a greater or lesser extent. It is not the case that you're either in Team Introvert or Team Extrovert and always have little in common with the other side and lots in common with your fellow 'teammates'.

4.3 There is more to personality than introversion

There's a second reason why it's so difficult to pin down exactly what an introvert looks and acts like. People are complex. Our character traits draw on several different areas, which together comprise our unique personality.

The MBTI profile, the first practical application of Jung's theories of introversion and extroversion, also includes three other personality dimensions to do with information-processing, decision-making, and dealing with the world. According to the MBTI tool, which side of each of these dimensions you prefer will influence your personality. A basic outline is in Figure 1. You can find more extensive descriptions at http://www.myersbriggs.org/my-mbti-personality-type/mbti-basics/.

According to the MBTI system, where you sit on each of these four dimensions affects your personality. It's scored as an either/or preference (so you'll come out as introvert OR extrovert, sensing OR intuitive by this model) resulting in 16 main personality types, but the framework acknowledges lots of variance within the types as well as between them.

The 'Big Five' theory of personality holds that there are five main dimensions of personality: extroversion, conscientiousness, agreeableness, openness, and neuroticism. According to this theory, it is the intersection of where we sit in each of the five main areas that governs our personality. This creates a multitude of possibilities about how we will feel and behave in any given situation, influenced by more than simply where we sit on the introvert/extrovert spectrum.

Whichever personality theory is in vogue, the important thing to remember is that there is a cocktail taking place when it comes to our personality: the combination of other traits or preferences, circumstances and upbringing will affect the 'sort' of introvert we are.

It can be tempting to further refine the introvert label, given that introverts are such a broad and varied tribe: you might consider yourself a sociable or a shy introvert, for example. But this list could be endless. It is more helpful to recognise that we are our own unique blend of characteristics, and that our upbringing and environment also have a role to play in how we see ourselves and act in the world.

In short: it isn't possible to spell out exactly how all introverts are – there is no such thing as an introvert blueprint.

Dimension	Primary question	Preference
Introversion/Extroversion	Where is your attention?	Introverts focus more on their internal world, extroverts focus more on the external world around them.
Sensing/iNtuiting	How do you take in information?	People with a sensing preference focus on basic information, those with an intuiting preference add meaning.
Thinking/Feeling	How do you make decisions?	'Thinkers' tend to favour logic and consistency, while 'Feelers' will focus on the particulars of a situation and the people involved.
Judging/Perceiving	How do you deal with the world?	People with a judging preference prefer to have their world more planned and ordered, while people with a perceiving preference prefer to adapt to the world around them.

Fig.1 The MBTI dimensions

4.4 Leveraging strengths for leadership

While you are your own unique self, with a different bundle of strengths and weaknesses to the introvert next door, there are attributes you are likely to have in common. These are strengths that may have been overlooked by yourself and your colleagues, in favour of the more outspoken traits displayed by extroverts.

Introversion & Leadership

Introverts in positions of leadership are in the minority – a large minority but a minority nevertheless. Our society is predisposed to reward and applaud more extroverted characteristics. But rather than this being a disadvantage for introverts, it can be a source of great power. Utilising the strengths that are more readily available to introverts in an environment that's not used to them is a little like having a superpower – you are using skills that many others don't possess or don't access readily.

What follows is a selection of qualities that many introverts possess, and which are real gifts when it comes to leadership. You may be surprised at some of these. They may run counter to traditional leadership attributes, or they may be skills that you didn't realise you possessed. But, used effectively, they are very powerful tools enabling you to be an authentic, effective leader.

Reflection

Introverts tend to deal in substance more than extroverts do. Rather than hover on the surface with small talk, introverts like to dive in and tussle with complex subjects. The thinking tends to be deeper and more focused. This is a result of all the internal processing that comes naturally to introverts – rather than bounce from one subject to another, introverts spend time thinking through the meaning and application of issues. So, while introverts might not be first to speak up in a meeting, or chip in with every discussion, what you contribute is likely to be valuable.

Embracing this, rather than feeling as though you have to make your presence felt with half-baked thoughts because everyone else is, will help you to cultivate this strength and focus your attention on what you're good at. You'll be recognised as someone worth listening to.

If you feel like you should say something before your thinking is complete – do. But be honest. Let your team or your boss know that you are developing your ideas and that they might be along certain lines, but you will outline them more fully in the next day or so.

Listening

It's too simplistic to categorise extroverts as natural talkers and introverts as natural listeners, but quieter people do tend to be good at listening. Listening - truly, actively listening, rather than waiting for the other person to finish so you can speak is a hugely undervalued skill.

Genuinely listening to someone is powerful. It builds relationships - people can tell when you are taking them seriously and will feel valued. It gives you insight – if you focus on the other person, rather than trying to defend your position, you'll gain new information or a new perspective. Combined with the ability to reflect, you may well find that listening opens up smarter ways of doing things than you'd first considered.

So, if you feel as though your leadership role means you should speak first and not heed dissenters in order to appear strong, remember the power of listening. Real strength lies in drawing on the information around you, taking the time to process it and changing course if need be.

Pause

Risk is often talked about as a hot leadership characteristic – and it's something more associated with extroverts, while introverts are stereotyped more as boring, change-resistant types. And while risk-taking can certainly be helpful in creating change and moving things forward, it's worth exploring the under-rated virtues of pausing when it comes to leadership.

Being a naturally more cautious person means you will pause before making decisions. You will look to gather evidence and be informed. You will ask searching questions. You will have your eyes wide open. This doesn't mean that you will never take a risk, it means your risks are more likely to be calculated. Which is a good thing. And importantly for leadership positions, it means that you can communicate your decisions clearly and effectively. The people reporting to you, and those you are accountable to, will all respect you more when they feel as though you have been honest and clear in your communication.

Planning

Introverts tend to get over-stimulated more easily, so thinking on the hoof may come less naturally. However, where introverts tend to shine is in their ability to deploy planning skills. Planning is a gift when it comes to meetings, networking or public speaking. It allows you to think ahead, focus on what's important and rehearse how you will behave.

The ability to plan is also useful in setting out and operationalising organisational goals. The introverted tendency to go deep with issues often translates into effective analytical skills: an ability to get to the heart of the matter and understand what is really important. These are highly valuable tools when it comes to forward planning, setting agendas, and making progress.

Many introverts are also more comfortable with writing than their extroverted counterparts. If this is you, then you have a valuable role in helping to communicate the purpose and objectives of your work and developing plans that help people understand their role in making things happen.

Quiet

Quiet is important for rest (true even for extroverts: most people prefer low-stimulation environments for sleeping, for example), for developing skills and for creativity. It's a powerful medium, one that has been under-valued in Western cultures that glorify concepts such as 'more' and 'busy'.

Research has shown that quiet is important for all of us if we want to deepen our expertise or tap into our creativity, but the great news for introverts is that we're more at home in quiet anyway.

Quiet allows us to concentrate. Research indicates that the best environments for focussed work have noise levels between 20 decibels and 60 decibels: around the volume of rustling leaves or low conversation. In most workplaces areas these noise levels are hard to come by, but you have every reason to seek them out. You will be more productive.

Solitude is also the way to get better at what you do, whether that's public speaking, engineering, coding, or tap dancing. Malcolm Gladwell, in his book 'Outliers', studied elites in a range of fields and found that the one unifying factor was the amount of time they had spent honing their craft – 10,000 hours was his magic number. And the practice had to be at the exact level needed for each individual, a sweet spot that challenged them enough so they pushed forward but didn't push too much too soon. And that sort of 'just right' practice tends to happen alone, in quiet.

As a leader, it's important for you to build quiet into your day so you can focus on the important things, see the wood for the trees and invest in yourself. And your affinity with quiet can also help those around you. The ability to be calm when others are stressed, jostling for position, or desperate for their view to prevail is very powerful. Being calm can diffuse conflict, bring clarity to discussion, and role-model a respectful approach to work.

Embracing your strengths

Don't be concerned if you don't feel you hold all of these strengths, or if there are strengths you draw on that aren't discussed here. The most important thing is to tune into what you are good at, and use that to your advantage. Do not assume that because you take a skill for granted, it isn't a strength you can bring to your leadership. Many of us don't pay attention to our strengths, assuming most others possess them too. This is often not the case.

If you'd like to explore your strengths more, take a free assessment here: http://www.viacharacter.org/www/.

Don't feel that because you may not match the characteristics traditionally associated with a charismatic, bold-talking, risk-taking leadership persona that your strengths aren't useful or effective in your leadership role. Quite the opposite.

4.5   Strengthening yourself

In the next chapter we discuss specific strategies you can use in a leadership role to navigate challenges. Underlying all of these practical approaches are the important dual principles of self-knowledge and self-respect.

It's important to cultivate a healthy, positive attitude to yourself and your abilities. This isn't about being arrogant or domineering, it is about developing the trust in yourself that you need to do your work well.

EXERCISE

Make it a habit to write down how you have made a positive impact, and the skills you have brought to your work and those around you. Create time and space for it in your calendar.

Use prompts such as:
'Today I used x strengths'
'Today I achieved…'
'If I had not done x, y would not have happened'
'I am closer to my goal today because of…'

Doing this daily or weekly will remind you of what you have to offer, help you to tap into those strengths when similar situations crop up, and provide a useful record if you need to boost your confidence or clearly demonstrate your worth to others at a meeting or interview.

4.6   Helping others

Given that we live in a society that tends to make extrovert assumptions about how the world works best, for example with drinks after work to help everyone relax and meetings as the most effective way of getting things done, it's worth thinking about what you can influence in your work culture to make things more comfortable for other introverts.

Introversion & Leadership

As a leader, you can influence what happens or how it happens in your work. Use this influence to leverage the strengths of all of those around you by compensating for standard practices that favour extroverts.

For example, ensure your meetings have agendas, with papers circulated in advance, and give people time after the meeting to reflect before responding. Adopting as many of these introvert-friendly practices as possible will enable the quieter amongst your team to shine, without stepping on the toes of your extroverted colleagues.

Key points

- You do not have any fixed capabilities: introversion is a preference but does not restrict you.
- Most introverts and extroverts are not poles apart, as many of us sit more to the middle of the spectrum.
- There is no blueprint to being an introvert. Many other dimensions of personality are at play in shaping personality traits, such as how we process information, make decisions, or interact with the world.
- Many introverts possess undervalued strengths, such as the ability to reflect, listen, pause before acting, and be comfortable with quiet. These are highly powerful in leadership.
- Understanding your strengths and reminding yourself of them is vital to effective leadership.
- As a leader, you are able to make changes to help other people as well as yourself, so introverts around you can deploy their skills more effectively.

5 Day to Day Strategies

As an introvert in a leadership role you have many opportunities to play to your strengths. You'll also need to work around, minimise or find ways to cope with situations that don't suit you. Recognising your value is foundational to this. If you are constantly feeding your mind with negative self-talk and convincing yourself that you don't have what it takes, you are working against yourself from the start.

Hopefully reading through the previous chapter on leveraging your strengths will have given you some ideas to build and preserve your sense of self-worth. What follows are some specific, practical strategies shared by fellow introverts to help you navigate potentially challenging situations.

5.1 Managing energy

The Challenge

As introverts, we often become overstimulated by busy lifestyles or environments. Introverts typically recharge in solitude, or quiet settings, and that is not always possible. Your office may be noisy, your working day is likely to involve meetings with others and your schedule may be jam-packed. As a leader, you may also be expected to work longer hours, or attend evening social and networking events. These situations are all likely to sap an introvert's energy.

Low energy can mean low leadership performance: if you tune out of conversations you risk missing information or coming across as disinterested, jeopardising personal or professional relationships. It is also simply not good for you to run on empty! To maintain your health and wellbeing, it's important to find ways to replenish your energy.

Hints and Tips from Other Introverts

Manage your time

If you are able to be flexible with your working day, try coming in early or leaving late to ensure you get some quieter time in your workplace - but balance this so you don't end up working extra long days.

Schedule meetings with at least a half hour break in between to have some time to yourself and to prepare.

At the end of each day identify the most important things you need to work on the following day and leave your desk ready to get started on it. Many leaders fall into the trap of checking emails first thing, but that can distract us and get our minds running off in hundreds of different directions – which can be particularly problematic for introverts who get easily over-stimulated. Instead, get straight to your priority tasks and focus on completing them. This will energise you for the rest of the day, and leave you confident that whatever else happens, at least you have got something important done.

If possible, set aside specific time to manage your emails. Setting aside time will help you consider emails as a specific task to get through, rather than a constant drip, drip, drip throughout your day that you notice but may not deal with. The old management adage of 'deal with/delete/delegate' is your friend here – try to make sure you take one of these actions against every email you get.

Manage your space

If you have workspace to yourself, set it up so that it suits you: you don't need to keep an open-door policy for your team. Instead set times when they are welcome to drop-in, or have regular one-to-one meetings.

Some introverts find that order, and surrounding themselves with well-chosen things that lift their mood helps them work well. Anna, a mental health specialist, says:

> "It matters a lot to me to be in an environment which is calm, aesthetically pleasing and functional."

Build in energy-boosts

Whether we are leaders in our workplaces, communities, or homes, there will be multiple pulls on our time, and culturally, we often feel as though we should just keep going. Personal energy experts Tony Schwartz and Catherine McCarthy have identified four areas where we are likely to experience energy depletion: body, mind, emotions, and spirit. Introverts are especially likely to feel drained more quickly in busy environments, so it's important to take responsibility for our own self-care.

Introversion & Leadership

Area	Key actions to boost energy.
Body	Prioritise sleep and regular healthy eating. Find ways to build physical activity into your day.
Mind	Allow yourself 90-minute stretches to focus fully, without interruption from people, email or phone. Distraction can cost around 25% of the total working time if you are always multitasking.
Emotions	Practice deep abdominal breathing to buy time before responding to difficult situations. Pay attention to what you can control and focus on being proactive.
Spirit	Develop daily habits that enable you to do the things you value most – both at work and at home. Anna finds that, "Ironically one of my most recharging activities is singing in a choir over 300 strong. We're engaged in a common enterprise and the results are amazing."

Ensure you take lunch – and take it alone or with a trusted person who won't drain your energy. Taking breaks during the working day may seem like slacking, but it's quite the opposite. It will help you function better.

Choose your work wisely

Some people make career changes to suit their energy levels and personality preferences. Rosanne, a copywriter, says that becoming director of her own creative agency was one of the best decisions she's made: "A lot of people don't think introversion is a good trait for a business owner but for me it's a huge asset. I get my best work done alone for hours on end, letting my mind go wild."

When considering changing jobs, or industries, take into account how the work will affect your energy. Nothing is off-limits to introverts, but if you choose a job that involves a lot of high-energy meetings, networking, and long hours around other people you will need to find more ways to replenish.

In your current job, think about the tasks that give you most energy. And think about the ones that drain you. Are there other people who could do these? This isn't about passing on the 'worst' jobs to other people, but recognising that different tasks suit different people better. As a leader, you are likely to manage others, whether they report directly to you or not. Are there people who would relish the projects or activities that make you wilt? Not only will you preserve your energy with judicious delegating, you'll boost your relationship with your team if you can find ways to give them work that they enjoy too.

5.2 Leading others

The Challenge

Introverts can be excellent people leaders - they usually have natural strengths to draw on such as listening, empathy, planning, analysis, little appetite for posturing, and a focus on objectives. But introverted leaders can also sometimes come off as aloof, indecisive, or controlling.

Susan Cain outlines how the twentieth century business world became dominated by 'personality': colourful, loud characters who were naturals at selling with their quick wit and social ease. This stereotype is still powerful, with many introverts feeling that they need to act as a charismatic extrovert to prove their authority.

However, the best leaders are those who can be themselves – they are naturally authoritative and operate with integrity. This applies equally to introverts and extroverts. Keri Potts, Senior Director of Public Relations at ESPN puts it like this:

"I've never bought into the concept of 'wearing the mask'. As a leader, the only way I know how to engender trust and buy-in from my team and with my colleagues is to be 100 percent authentically me—open, sometimes flawed, but always passionate about our work. It has allowed me the freedom to be fully present and consistent. They know what they're getting at all times. No surprises."

Hints and Tips from Other Introverts

Build a diverse team

As Kay, a team leader for an environmental organisation, notes, "In the workplace, diversity gets better decisions." It may be tempting to surround yourself with people closely matched to you: meetings will be less rowdy, people will provide thought through responses to your questions, you are likely to agree more often than you disagree.

But it's important that your team includes a wide range of personality types, extroverts included. Your decisions will be better for being tested, and you can draw on the strengths of your extroverts in areas where you are less comfortable: empowering an extroverted deputy to front a campaign or presentation, for example.

Communicate effectively

It may be tempting for introverted leaders to shut themselves away and converse with their team via email. While it is possible to work like this, without any face-to-face or telephone contact you risk dis-engaging your team, especially the extroverts.

But neither do you need high-powered, large group inspirational meetings to be an effective communicator. Just make time to see the people you work with every so often. Collette, a writer, says "Don't try to be loud and extrovert, but do be firm and believe in yourself, even if you're doing it quietly. That inner belief projects itself well."

It's important your team know what you expect of them. Introverts have rich inner worlds, and it's possible to forget to share what's in our heads. Be clear about work objectives and office protocols, ensuring everything is in writing for later reference.

Nurture relationships

Introverts tend to be leaders that build trust in smaller settings. So make sure you get to know your direct reports well. Katrina, a marketing specialist, suggests, "Have regular one-to-ones and show something of yourself so they see you are a person too."

Rather than relying on charisma, introverts can make excellent facilitative leaders: a leadership style which places the team front and centre, rather than their own egos. Encouraging an environment where your team can share their ideas, know they will be listened to, and know that credit will be shared with the team rather than hogged by the leader is an effective way to mobilise high performance, and plays to a typical introvert preference to stay out of the limelight.

Delegate

Introverts tend not to delegate as much as extroverts; it may be that we want to retain full control, or we feel awkward about burdening others. Whatever the reason, the ability to delegate is important: it helps prevent burnout, and it can be a highly effective way of getting buy-in as you are demonstrating your faith in your colleague's abilities.

When delegating a project, brief the person you are giving it to by making clear why they are picking it up. Specifically, be clear about:

- Why it needs doing: how does this support your organisation's work?
- What needs doing: what does the completed project look like? How much freedom will they have?
- Why them: this might be something mundane because they have the most availability, or it may be they have particular skills to bring.

De-escalate conflict

Conflict can arise anywhere, but the different communication preferences of introverts and extroverts can be a particular source of frustration. While extroverts may relish 'verbal jousting' and not feel wounded by robust discussion, introverts may see this as aggressive and often prefer to avoid situations where conflict may arise.

Gill, an assistant director at a university, notes how her team members were often griping with each other over seemingly trivial issues, such as office doors being left open, before they had a team away day focussed on their preferences as described in the MBTI tool. Once everyone had become aware of their own and their colleagues' preferences, they took differences less personally, and were able to come up with solutions.

If you find yourself in conflict with another person, or managing conflict within your team, your introversion is immensely powerful. Draw on your preference for calm to cool the situation down:

- Prepare in advance if you can. Look at things from both sides so you can anticipate objections and find a way forward, either by overcoming the objection or modifying your stance.
- Don't get drawn into the heat. Allow time for silence or paraphrase their arguments to give you time to process them, and to check your understanding.
- Look for points of agreement, e.g., "We both agree we need to change our email system. What's the most important thing to you?"
- Get both sides to take responsibility and find solutions. This isn't a battle to be won, but an answer to be found. An introvert's analytical, objective approach can help put the work issue at the centre of the discussion, rather than people's egos.

5.3 Meetings

The Challenge

Whether you're chairing or simply attending, meetings can be tough environments for introverts. You may feel like you need to speak up but can't get a word in, or you may feel like decisions are made without enough time for discussion or reflection. When it comes down to who has the loudest voice or the most persuasive arguments at their fingertips, introverts may feel disadvantaged. But, handled well, the focus, calm and listening skills that your introversion bring can make you highly effective round the table.

Hints and Tips from Other Introverts

Prepare

More than anything else, this is the top tip from introverts when it comes to meetings. Of course, if schedules are frantic, this can be difficult, but it is worth creating good habits. What wastes more time: half an hour's preparation scheduled in the day before your meeting (even five minutes just before if you're really pushed), or bad decisions and lost opportunities because you weren't ready to speak up?

If you are attending a meeting, preparation time will enable you to work out where you want to contribute and influence, and research any evidence needed to back up your points. You may also want to talk to other meeting attendees in advance, to brief them on your arguments. If you are trying to influence an outcome, doing this has two advantages: it allows you to test your arguments in a one-to-one setting, refining them if need be, and it can help you gain allies to your cause.

If you are chairing, preparation time will help you clarify the purpose and desired outcomes for the meeting, so you can keep things on track and take the chair with authority. It's useful to use a three-point framework for each agenda item:

- Information: make the purpose of the agenda item clear, e.g. "We will decide which team will represent us at the conference this year".
- Discussion: let the debate flow, ensuring you stick to time.
- Outcome: whether this is a final decision, a referral to another meeting or a request for more information, make sure the outcome of the item is clear before moving on. Beth, a team leader for a global scientific company, makes a point of following up the meeting by email: "I always send out notes to clarify the discussions and decisions so that everyone has clear direction."

Participate

Having faith that what you have to contribute needs to be heard can be the motivation you need to speak up – which is another reason why preparation is so important. As Dean, a marketing executive, puts it, "If you feel you have something of genuine value to contribute, then it's your duty to speak up." Choose the points you particularly want to make, and get your voice heard.

If there are items that you don't have strong feelings on, it's helpful to contribute in other ways. Use non-verbal communication to show you are listening. Collette suggests, "Demonstrate you are engaged with lots of smiling, nodding, frowning etc, even if you don't say much."

Let everyone speak
This includes you! If you get cut off or talked over by the louder members of your meeting, politely return to your point with a bridging statement along the lines of: "Thanks Heather – as I was saying…"

As an introverted leader you are well placed to create space for the other introverts in the group to contribute. If possible, build in quiet time within the meeting, such as a few minutes to review a report, or a short break to enable introverts to gather their thoughts before contributing. If timings allow, you could offer attendees the opportunity to email any additional thoughts after the meeting, before making a final decision.

5.4 Presentations and public speaking

The Challenge
Public speaking can be a daunting prospect for anyone. Introverts, who tend to thrive in quieter environments and smaller groups can find themselves particularly unnerved by being in front of a large audience. And there is the practical problem of communicating the message effectively too: how do you convey a message effectively and enthusiastically if you naturally have a quieter style?

Hints and Tips from Other Introverts

Prepare
Preparation was the number one tip for handling meetings effectively, and it's doubly true here. As Rosanne puts it, "As long as you believe in what you are saying and know your subject well it's ok, because the attention is on the subject matter and not you."

Malcolm Gladwell, author, speaker, and introvert, is clear that "Speaking is not an act of extroversion". He describes it as a performance, and to do his performance well (which he does), he prepares thoroughly through scripting and rehearsing his speeches, so that when he delivers them he does so naturally and with confidence.

Be audience-focused
A key element of preparation is understanding who you are talking to, and what will engage them. You might want to secure a contract to provide meals to a school: the same presentation won't work for parents, the school management team, and the children.

So, consider your key message carefully, and think about what evidence or anecdotes you can offer to ensure your audience cares about it as much as you do.

This element of public speaking – considering others and planning carefully – plays to many introverts' strengths, enabling them to craft compelling arguments.

Be yourself
Just as with leading people, the key to success with presentations lies in being comfortable with yourself. If you are not naturally a wildly gesticulating, emotional sort of speaker, don't try to be. You can relax into your performance knowing that you have prepared well. But let your conviction in what you are saying come through with a quiet authority that is naturally your own – it will be more powerful in its authenticity.

5.5 Networking and socialising

The Challenge
Traditionally, business networking involves settings that are draining and uncomfortable for introverts: breakfast or evening soirées, business trips involving socialising and small talk, conference dinners where the real deals are done. For people who prefer smaller groups and deeper conversation rather than small talk and working the room, networking, and socialising can become a dreaded chore.

Hints and Tips from Other Introverts
Give yourself time to recharge
If you need to attend networking meetings or a business trip, don't be afraid to give yourself breaks from the noisy hub. Ways to escape include:
- Use breaks in the programme to take a walk, alone, or with a trusted colleague.
- Take work, or reading material, on journeys, so you can politely let your neighbour know that you need to focus on that rather than chat through the entire flight or train journey.
- Turn down some social engagements: if you're on a work trip, you don't need to have drinks with your colleagues every night. Think quality, not quantity.

Set goals
Be aware of your energy levels so you know how much you can take. You might find it useful to set targets for yourself: give yourself permission to leave the breakfast networking session after you've spoken to three people, or target the people you particularly want to meet. If you have personal contacts who know someone you'd like to get to know, ask for an introduction to ease your way in.

Integrating into a new network is often a matter of 'little and often' for introverts, who have lots to contribute but prefer not to do it in a showy way. So, a good tactic is to turn up to the same networks regularly, but don't feel bad about leaving when you feel your energy wane.

Focus on others, not yourself
Introverts tend to be great listeners. Enter the social fray armed with some questions to get you started:
- "What's been the highlight of your week?"
- "What did you think about the keynote speech?"
- "When's your next holiday?"

A few well-placed questions are often enough to carry the conversation. It's even better if you can use what you find out to help your fellow networkers – maybe you can forward a report, put them in touch with a useful contact, or let them pick your brains. Being helpful is a great way to get noticed and remembered.

Do it your own way
You may find you can avoid big networking events entirely and make connections in your own way. Jo, an online entrepreneur, says, "I say no to a lot of networking, it hasn't held me back. I would rather go for coffee with one person and make a meaningful connection."

If it's possible for you to connect with people in ways you find more comfortable, do it. Ask potential collaborators, allies, or clients to meet one-to-one rather than try to corner them at a busy evening event.

Digital networking offers scope for 'meeting' people that is helpful for introverts too. Use LinkedIn to find articles or groups that interest you and start by 'liking' or 'upvoting' the content in there that resonates with you. Getting to know someone through their work is a great way to form a connection.

And remember that effective networking is not about making as many contacts as you can. It's about making meaningful connections. So it's perfectly legitimate to seek out opportunities to meet where you are at your most natural, high energy and authentic.

5.6 Office environment

The Challenge
It's not always possible to choose our working environment. Offices can be busy, noisy, shared workspaces that challenge introverts who prefer quiet focus.

Introversion & Leadership

Extroverts, who often prefer to 'chew things over' or simply chat to stay energised may not realise what a drain they are being on their introvert colleagues. As leaders, we may have more freedom over our workspace, if not, we certainly have the right to set out the conditions we need to work effectively: we have a responsibility to our team and our own leaders to be on top form.

Hints and Tips from Other Introverts
Be clear about when you're off-limits

If you have your own office, it's worth setting communication protocols. Gill says, "My team knew that if my office door was closed, it meant I didn't want to be interrupted, except for an emergency. An open door meant they were free to drop by." Instead of an open-door policy you might want to set hours where you're available, and ask people to contact you during that time.

If you share an office, particularly if it's open plan, you'll have to work harder to carve out uninterrupted time. Signs, colour-codes and earphones are all tactics you can use to let people know when you're available and when you want to keep your head down. Beth says "I work in an open plan office, which is a struggle sometimes, but my earphones are close by when needed. I am also comfortable saying "can I get back to you later?"

Be honest

Not everyone is aware that other people have different needs. Rather than get frustrated by the constant background chatter, it's worth telling your office companions that it's helpful for you to work in quiet, and negotiate times of the day that are quieter.

Go elsewhere

Schedule in some time each week when you work from home, or from a quieter environment, such as an unused meeting room or a local coffee shop. It will help you focus on your work without distraction from other people, emails, and routine phone calls.

Key Points

Challenge	Strategies
Managing your energy in a busy workplace	Build in quiet time. Arrange your space so it helps rather than hinders. Focus on what you can control. Take basic self-care seriously: eat and sleep well. Choose work that fulfils you.
Leading others when you are naturally more of a 'closed book'	Build a diverse team to embrace others' strengths, and delegate accordingly. Nurture relationships. Communicate effectively, backing things up in writing. Use your natural calm and ability to listen to de-escalate conflict
Chairing and participating in meetings	Prepare your thoughts and approach in advance. Participate, using non-verbal communication if nothing else. Don't allow yourself to be talked over. Notice the other introverts and include them.
Giving presentations and public speaking	Prepare thoroughly. Remember the attention is on your message not on you. Be audience-focussed – relate your message to them. Rehearse so you can be more relaxed. Don't try to be someone you're not.
Networking and socialising	Take breaks. Set manageable goals. Be a great listener and help your contacts. Do it differently: set up one-to-one meetings. Network online using LinkedIn and other social media.
Coping with a busy office environment	Have some 'off-limits' time: shut your door, schedule drop-in time, use earplugs or signs. Be honest and clear about your needs with colleagues to negotiate a solution that suits everyone. Work elsewhere when you can.

6 Working with Extroverts

6.1 A word of warning

Much of this book so far has extolled the virtues of introverts. And there are many. It's important to realise the strengths an introverted preference offers, and to make full use of them in your leadership role.

But it's also important not to overcompensate. Recent research tells us that introverted brains have more going on neurologically. They spend more time reflecting and considering. But this does not mean that introverts are more intelligent, or that extroverts are shallow. Extroverts are just as capable of being creative, finding solutions and providing insight. They just get there differently.

In embracing your own way of doing things, it's important not to look down on the approaches of others. Just as you are ignoring a valuable resource if you dismiss your own strengths, you risk alienating and neglecting important resources if you undermine those who approach the world differently.

6.2 The value of extroverts

It's as impossible to provide an extrovert blueprint as it is to provide an introvert one – we are all unique and complex creatures. But it is worth remembering some of the strengths that extroverts bring. Amongst other things, extroverts tend to:

- Have great verbal skills – they can speak up and respond 'on the hoof', which is helpful if you're looking for initial feedback or someone to bounce ideas around with.
- Network and socialise with lots of people. Rather than the quiet, more targeted opportunities for networking that introverts prefer, extroverts have a wide social circle. This can be useful in picking up ideas and news on the grapevine.
- Act quickly and with energy. If you are looking to get something off the ground, the enthusiasm and risk-taking extroverts are likely to be allies in gathering momentum and giving it a go.

6.3 Diversity as a winning formula

If you surround yourself only with people who think and behave as you do, you miss the opportunity to draw on new perspectives.

Your product, service, idea, or cause needs as much input as you can gather and will be stronger for being tested by people who don't see the world your way. As Kay tells us, "Some of my best friends are extroverts and I love them for it. In a work setting diversity gets better decisions."

Jennifer Kahnweiler is an extroverted author who has written about the value of introverts and extroverts working together in her book *The Genius of Opposites*. She outlines her *ABCDE* formula for getting the most out of working with people of the opposite preference:

The ABCDE Approach

Accept the **A**lien: Understand that there are other ways of doing things. Not better or worse than yours, just different.

Bring on the **B**attles: Be prepared to disagree and know that, handled well, disagreements will bring stronger solutions.

Cast the **C**haracter: Play to your strengths. If you have an extrovert who loves conferences while you don't, divide the work accordingly.

Destroy the **D**islike: Once you can see the value of your opposite, you can have a more positive and productive working relationship.

Each can't offer **E**verything: Remember that diversity is the best way to deliver on your objectives.

6.4 Nurture who you have

As a leader you have a responsibility to achieve the vision you, or others, have set out. The very best way to do this is to draw on all the resources you have available as effectively as possible. You will make your job far harder if you insist on just one way of doing things.

Good leadership is responsive, not dictatorial. It's important to be clear in setting the direction so people understand what they need to achieve and what's expected of them. But, recognise that people are different, and give them the freedom to work in ways that suit them best.

In Chapter Three (Myths and Stereotypes) we saw that one of the traits of effective leadership is allowing people to self-organise. Doing this, rather than micromanaging, enables people both to develop ownership of their work and to use the strategies that work best for them.

It is sometimes obvious what other people's preferences are, especially once you have spent time understanding and accepting your own. Don't assume that everyone else has the same level of self-awareness. Think about the people you work with on a regular basis. Does your leadership style and the work culture you are part of allow them to play to their strengths?

Perhaps you are working with people who feel trapped into doing things a certain way, because that's the way it's always been: introverts who wouldn't dream of seeking out a quiet place away from the shared office to focus on a report, or extroverts who are bored with running the same events in the same old ways.

Giving people options is a positive leadership move. It demonstrates respect for your colleagues and they are likely to deepen their respect for you in return. It also means you are likely to achieve your goals more easily as people will be working more effectively and will be happier doing what comes naturally.

If it is difficult to tell what preferences your colleagues have, or if you sense conflict due to personality clashes, give them the opportunity to do a little self-analysis. If you don't have the resources to get a trained coach or facilitator to support you, try these steps:

1. Either in a meeting or by email, let your team know that you would like to create a working environment that plays to everyone's strengths, and for everyone to feel respected. If a specific conflict has triggered this, be honest about wanting to address it, while not blaming anyone involved.

2. Introduce the idea of introversion and extroversion preferences. The Myers-Briggs Foundation has a helpful summary available online:
http://www.myersbriggs.org/my-mbti-personality-type/mbti-basics/extraversion-or-introversion.htm

3. Share an online assessment with everyone involved. There are many available. This one is thorough in the questions and the analysis you receive as a result (the same assessment as suggested in Chapter Two, What Is Introversion?):
https://www.16personalities.com

4. Set a time for debriefing. Reinforce the key messages that one type is not better than another, and that diversity in the team is a great strength. Don't force people to share their preferences, but you can remind them that understanding each other will lead to a more harmonious, productive and respectful workplace.

5. Give people the opportunity to feedback their thoughts, either at a group meeting or by email. They may have suggestions on how to change work practices, their own schedule or how they interact with you as a result of their new understanding. Be open to these ideas. They may include requests to work from home more often, to have fewer or more meetings, to have quiet and chatty times in the day.

6. When deciding to make or allow changes based on people's preferences, set a trial period. This is useful to make sure you don't get locked into work practices that turn out to be unhelpful, but also to keep preferences as a 'live' issue. They will be likely to pay attention to their own styles and those of their colleagues knowing that there will be a review coming up.

6.5 Communicate your own needs

As we come to the end of this chapter, it's important to remember your own needs. If you work with a large and mixed team it's simply not realistic for you to accommodate every individual preference: Annie might like daily five minute face-to-face meetings, Bob might want an open door policy so he can talk ideas through, Connie might ask for two weeks' notice before every meeting or new request, David would like to work from home all of the time but needs to liaise with Bob who likes to chat face-to-face…

It is not your job to make things perfect for everybody. However, it is helpful for you, and productive for your colleagues, if you are able to create a respectful work environment that takes account of everyone's preferences, including your own. But that doesn't mean you are able to create a tailored workplace for each individual.

It might be that you decide on some principles for your workplace, such as an open-door policy between 9.30 – 10.30am and 1-3pm allowing people to drop by, but protecting quieter working outside that time. Maybe you can set up quiet zones at work, where people know they will be able to work in silence and without interruption.

Being honest about your own preferences, and the strengths you bring will help other people do the same. Recognising that other people have different strengths (and that includes fellow introverts as well as the extroverts) will help them value their skills and the contributions they make.

Key Points

- It's important not to diminish the value of extroverts when embracing introvert strengths: labelling all extroverts as shallow or less insightful is a mistake.
- Extroverts have many strengths that effective leaders are wise to recognise and draw on, such as networking and verbal skills, and a positive attitude to change.
- Diversity in your team is a powerful asset. The ABCDE approach enables you to acknowledge and respect different ways of working.
- Effective leaders give people room to work well, and to develop. Nurture self-awareness in your team and help them to understand their preferences.
- While respecting others, remember to look after your own needs and maintain boundaries to help you work effectively.

7 Pitfalls and Watchouts

By now, it should be clear that introverted tendencies in a leadership role are not a handicap, and can be an advantage in many ways, especially when you are aware of your preferences. A note of caution, however, there are traps you can fall into.

7.1 Overplaying your strengths

In Chapter Four (Uniquely You), we looked at five strengths that are more readily accessible to most introverts. These strengths are sometimes overlooked, but as we have discussed, can be hugely helpful in leadership.

There is a shadow side to each of these attributes though. Balance is what is called for. Let's take each of them in turn:

Reflection

Used wisely, your ability to turn things over in your mind can be a huge asset when it comes to problem solving, creativity, or strategic thinking. But don't let reflection become rumination. In psychological terms, rumination is the act of obsessing or overthinking situations.

Introverts are more prone to rumination than extroverts as they often deal in meaning and concept, growing thoughts in their minds, rather than dealing solely with the external world. It can lead to harmful thought patterns, such as catastrophising, or overplaying negative aspects of a situation while ignoring the positives. This can lead to poor self-respect if you are ruminating about yourself, or a tunnel-visioned approach if you are trying to understand a situation or your colleagues.

If you tend to ruminate, try and brings things back to a more concrete level. Rather than speculate about what might happen, focus on specific things – good and bad. It can be helpful to ask a trusted colleague (perhaps an extrovert) to share their perspective, to broaden out your own thoughts.

Pitfalls and Watchouts

Listening

Listening is important for building relationships and in gathering information to help you in your work. Given how frequently people use a discussion purely to state their own view without stopping to consider and assimilate what the other person has said, the ability to listen well can truly be called a superpower.

But don't be a doormat. One of the consequences of listening is that you are likely to hear differences of opinion. People will view the world differently and that is to be expected. You will not be able to solve everyone's problems or come up with a solution that pleases everybody. Your role, as a leader, is to use what you have heard to take action with integrity.

When listening, especially if you are listening to opinions you have sought out, make it clear that you will take on board what the other person is saying, but will make your own decision. Set parameters around what you will do with the information or opinion you hear. Effective listening involves effective communication, so make sure you set expectations, decisions, and objectives out clearly.

Pause

The ability to pause is a wonderful skill that helps you be better informed and not get swept away by groupthink or the latest trend. As a result, you're more likely to make sound decisions and communicate them effectively, gaining the respect of those around you.

Over-caution, though, is a risk in itself. You risk losing opportunities for yourself or your work's objectives. You also risk the relationship with colleagues who are excited by change. If you feel that you are a little over-cautious in your approach to life and work, try these strategies:

- Write a risk assessment for the scenario – don't just keep it in your head. Picture the risks clearly and face them head on. Sometimes the practical act of putting your concerns on paper, thinking about how likely they are to happen, and what the consequences might be is enough to help you understand where caution is legitimate, and where there is room to take a calculated risk.
- Seek out a coach or mentor to discuss situations with. Talking with someone you trust who is not personally invested in your work is a helpful way to get a fresh perspective and test out ideas and concerns.
- Build a safety net. If you are worried about the 'what-ifs', put contingencies in place that will make things easier if the worst did happen. Taking out home contents insurance is an example of this. You could sketch out plans B and C in advance so you have peace of mind that you can handle things if the original risk didn't work out as you'd hoped.

Introversion & Leadership

Planning

Planning is an important stage in completing something well. Effective planning can help you prepare for a meeting, a presentation, or a conference. However you also need to *attend* the meeting, presentation, or conference. Without following through on your planning your efforts are wasted.

Don't use planning as a procrastination tool or as a way of hiding from the world. Introverts who are skilled at analysis and writing can spend weeks honing plans, creating beautiful documents or spreadsheets and nuancing their message. Thinking things through in advance and articulating them well is valuable, but action also needs to take place. There is a time to let things go and put them out into the world.

Quiet

As we have seen, quiet is helpful for everybody, including extroverts. Introverts are more at home in quiet as they don't require the same level of external stimulation as extroverts.

But quiet isn't always where the action is, and sometimes you need to be where the action is. Your leadership role will require it of you, either through convention (because in your industry leaders are expected to attend conferences, for example) or through your work's purpose. As a leader your job is to take your work forward, whether that's a cause, an organisation, or a specific project. This will involve being out there, in the world, in some form.

You can use the strategies discussed in Chapter Five (Day to Day Strategies) to create moments of quiet when you are in more stimulating environments: build in regular breaks and make sure you have time to yourself during a business trip, for example.

You can also deploy what Susan Cain calls 'Free Trait Theory'. She describes how some introverts in leadership positions are able to adopt extroverted personas when they need to: as gregarious party guests, charismatic and entertaining public speakers, or sociable hosts.

And while they will still need quiet time to recover, they don't find it particularly stressful. Cain argues this is because many introverts are able to tune in to their extroverted side, particularly when they are engaged in something they value highly. So, the quiet administrator becomes a fundraising whirlwind when he's supporting a cause he cares about. Or the quiet leader delivers a compelling, heartfelt speech arguing for a new approach.

Recognise and embrace your love of quiet. It is important and it can be the source of much creativity, innovation, wisdom, and calm. But don't forget to be in the world too.

7.2 Don't box yourself in

We have seen how introversion/extroversion is a dimension of personality. It is one dimension of many, and it is a spectrum. It is also a preference, not a cast in stone capability. You do not sit within an introvert box. Think of it more as being in a library, with some behavioural traits housed on the higher shelves, slightly more out of reach than others.

Jung held that people do best when they can move along the introvert/extrovert continuum as needed. He also postulated that people moved more to the centre of the spectrum and were more likely to tap into their 'other side' as they grew older and more comfortable with themselves.

So, as you embrace your introverted preference and the gifts it brings, don't neglect opportunities to stretch yourself and try extroverted approaches every so often. Another of the leadership qualities we discussed in Chapter Three (Myths and Stereotypes) was being open to learning: trying new things, looking for opportunities to grow, and keeping an open mind.

Introverted types are naturally a little more cautious than extroverts, and doing something differently might not come as naturally. This is all the more reason to push yourself. Einstein is famously attributed with saying that insanity is "doing the same thing over and over again and expecting different results". Adopting a spirit of curiosity will enable you to try new things, experiment with approaches and move along the introversion/extroversion more readily, as the situation requires.

Key points

- Your strengths are an asset, but can be a weakness if not balanced with action.
- Don't let reflection become rumination, don't let listening prevent you from making clear decisions, don't let planning and pause become procrastination or a preference for quiet become a way to hide from the world.
- Introversion and extroversion are on a spectrum. Jung held that people operate best when they can move up and down the spectrum, rather than be boxed in as a type.
- Openness to learning is an important leadership quality. Allow yourself to try different ways of doing things and remind yourself that your preference is not a restriction. It is a starting point for self-awareness.

8 Conclusion

What we achieve inwardly will change outer reality - Plutarch

Plutarch's words are a gift to introverts, with our rich inner worlds, depth, and focus. But they are true for everyone. The ability to be an effective leader, wherever you are on the introversion/extroversion spectrum starts with your mindset.

We have seen how Western culture society expects extroverts to do better, sets up schools and workplaces so people with a more externally focussed attitude will thrive, and that even introverts themselves regard extroversion as being 'better'.

We have also seen how leadership qualities such as acting with integrity, empowering others, communicating effectively and being open to learning are neither 'extrovert' or 'introvert' characteristics. These are behaviours that any leader can work on.

Introverted leaders truly have much to offer, drawing on a calm, reflective approach to set out visionary ideas, effective plans and build strong relationships with others. Putting these skills to work involves embracing your quieter tendencies and taking the time to reflect on your strengths.

Some work practices may not be natural territory for introverts: the evening networking dinner, the need to be available to many people during the working day. But there are strategies you can adopt to prepare and equip yourself with the energy you need to perform well.

The most important action you can take as an introverted leader is to nurture your own strengths, and the strengths of those around you. Being successful in leadership is not a competition, at least not with anyone other than yourself. By understanding your own preferences more fully you will be able to tap into introverted qualities that set you apart as a self-assured, authentic leader with presence.

Your introversion isn't a box to feel trapped by, much less a negative way of being in the world. It is a powerful insight into how you work, and what you need to do to be at your best. Tap into your strengths and let you be you, in all your quiet glory.

Acknowledgements

This little book couldn't have come into being if Gayle Johnson of Red Tree Writing hadn't taken my chaotic thoughts and research and pulled it into words that made sense. And even then, the manuscript sat gathering e-dust on my hard drive until my talented daughter Gemma Harrop brought it to life through Kindle Direct Publishing. I'm immensely grateful to both.

I'm blessed with wonderful supportive daughters; Hazel Harrop was kind enough to lend me her sharp eyes to check for inconsistencies when I got too close to the manuscript to see them (any remaining errors of course are all mine). Jodie Harrop, youngest and fellow introvert, supports me more than she knows with her kind funny wisdom. And thank you to my extrovert husband Paddy, yang to my yin. I'm so proud of and love my family for just accepting me as I am.

I'm also grateful to the generous souls who answered my survey call for those who identify with introverted traits thereby providing the case study material throughout. I have of course used pseudonyms to protect individual identities, but I hugely appreciated hearing their stories and the generosity of their contribution.

Where next...?

Rachel has a small, quiet, closed Facebook group called Introvert by Nature created as a safe community space we can breathe out, embrace our introverted preferences, and be ourselves. The intention is for it to be a place to explore and enjoy all things quiet; to share experiences, thoughts, books, dreams, research, frustrations, scenes of beauty, must-see films... anything that makes our introvert souls sing with joy or nod in recognition. If this speaks to you, you're welcome to seek the group out on Facebook.

Rachel works 1:1 with a small number of private clients (not just introverts!), helping them to embrace their true nature and know that they are enough. Find out more on her website.

Details of any courses, webinars or retreats Rachel may be running can also be found on her website or via Facebook.

Find out more on:

Facebook
https://www.facebook.com/TeaAndEmpathyCoaching/

Introvert by Nature Facebook Group
https://www.facebook.com/groups/introvertbynature/

Rachel's Website
www.teaandempathy.com